MORE TO THE XTREME

by Joe Layden

SCHOLASTIC INC.

New York Toronto London Auckland Sydney
Mexico City New Delhi Hong Kong Buenos Aires

PHOTO CREDITS:
All photos, unless noted otherwise:
Icon Sports Media.

ISBN 0-439-38574-1

12 11 10 9 8 7 6 5 4 3 2 1 2 3 4 5 6 7/0

Printed in the U.S.A.
First Scholastic printing, April 2002
Book Design: Michael Malone

TABLE of CONTENTS

To Matthew Maher
—J.L.

INTRODUCTION

Imagine this...

A day in the summer of 1995, shortly before the very first edition of something known as the Extreme Games. Around the offices of ESPN, the sports programming network that will broadcast and promote the new event, some people are nervous. ESPN has made its reputation on the backs of such traditional sports as football and basketball. So why is the network messing around with...well, whatever this is?

Skateboarding?

BMX?

Freestyle motocross?

What's going on here, anyway?

"Some people wondered if this was what ESPN should be doing," Ron Semaio, one of the founders of the X Games, told EXPN.com. "They wondered if these were even legitimate sports. As it got closer to the first Games, a lot of people were hiding under their desks,

Ryan Nyquist

thinking it was going to be a total disaster."

Boy, were they wrong. Fans of alternative sports flooded the streets of Providence, Rhode Island, that summer. They lined up three deep along the street luge course. They waited hours for seats at other venues. And they weren't just kids, either. Entire families came to support these new athletes, and this new breed of sport. Some were just curious, of course. They had no idea what to expect. But many of them were athletes themselves, with a deep passion for the sports on display. For them, it was a chance to see the best in the world.

It was, in a sense, like a ticket to the Super Bowl.

Some alternative athletes would cringe at the idea of being compared to superstar athletes in the mainstream sporting world. Originally, the whole point of extreme sports was simply to have fun. To express your individuality and athleticism and creativity by participating in sports most people didn't recognize as sports. It wasn't about money and sponsors and television contracts. It wasn't even really about winning. A group of kids would get together in a parking lot somewhere, slap together a few makeshift ramps, and perform tricks on skateboards or bicycles. Just for the pure thrill of it.

That was extreme sports... back in the day.

Times have changed. The Extreme Games have become the X Games, a multimillion-dollar annual alternative sports festival. There's a Winter X Games now, too. And a second giant festival called the Gravity Games. There's wall-to-wall television coverage. There are dozens of magazines devoted to skateboarding, BMX, snowboarding, and

"The state of (alternative) sports is pretty crazy now. The level of competition, the seriousness, the money, the exposure. It's amazing just how popular they've become."
—Tony Hawk

other sports that once couldn't get a line in the newspaper. Check out the local Blockbuster or Hollywood, and you'll see a wall of videos featuring big-air hotshots, and scores of video games endorsed by the likes of skateboarding legend Tony Hawk and freestyle BMX star Dave Mirra.

In other words, what once was alternative has now become mainstream. Sporting goods stores stock skateboards and mountain bikes right alongside the baseball bats

Tony Hawk

and football helmets. And vert ramps are a common sight in playgrounds. If such commercialism goes against the rebel image of extreme sports, well, maybe that's not such a terrible thing. Millions of people—young and old—have embraced alternative sports. As a result, the equipment has gotten better and safer. And opportunities abound. No longer are these sports just for daredevils and acrobats. Anyone can skateboard or snowboard. Anyone can ride a bike.

All you need is the right attitude. (A sturdy helmet is still a good idea, though!)

If you're wondering how we arrived at this point, this book will provide something of a roadmap. For example, who invented the skateboard? Or the snowboard? Who had the bright idea of doing flips and jumps on a tiny bicycle, thus giving birth to the sport of freestyle BMX? And what about wakeboarding, that wild combination of water skiing, snowboarding, and surfing? Who dreamed that one up? And why?

The answers are here, and some of them might surprise you.

You'll also find profiles of many of the top athletes in alternative sports—from legends such as BMX pioneer Mat Hoffman to wakeboarding superstar Dallas Friday, who is only fourteen years old...and already an X Games champion.

CHAPTER 1

FREESTYLE BMX

If you want to stretch the definition, then freestyle BMX is the old-timer of alternative sports. Think about it. As long as there have been bicycles (and that's at least a couple hundred years), there have been riders, some of whom weren't content to glide safely down the road. Then, as now, they sometimes let go of the handlebars. They sought out jumps and obstacles.

2001 Gravity Games
RESULTS

Bike Vert

1. Jamie Bestwick
2. Kevin Robinson
3. Simon Tabron

"Bob Haro inspired the 'do it yourself' attitude that drives our sport. If it wasn't for him, I could very well not be here. He's one of my all-time heroes."
—Mat Hoffman

And they prompted others to shake their heads in wonder.

Of course, the tricks of the nineteenth century, like the bikes on which they were performed, bore only a passing resemblance to what you might see at a freestyle BMX competition today. But the heart of the sport remains unchanged. These athletes are driven by a love for riding and creating, and a need to push themselves to the limit.

The modern version of freestyle riding was born in the mid-1970s, when bicycle motocross racing was riding a wave of popularity. In BMX, as it was called, competitors raced small, lightweight bikes around a dirt track. Spills and crashes were common, as was spectacularly athletic and aggressive riding. Some riders would even perform jumps and other tricks when they no longer had a chance to win a race.

2001 X Games RESULTS

Bicycle Stunt Flatland

1. Martti Kuoppa
2. Phil Dolan
3. Matt Wilhelm

If there is one man who deserves credit for refining and promoting freestyle BMX, and perhaps even "creating" it, that man is Bob Haro. A skateboarder and BMX racer from southern California, Bob began taking his bike to the concrete skateparks near his home. His idea was to combine his two favorite sports: skateboarding and BMX. To that end, he modified his favorite skateboarding tricks and tried to re-create them on his bike.

(continued on page 26)

star profile

DATE OF BIRTH: JANUARY 9, 1972

"I've never really had a plan. I just adapted what riding taught me and carried it over to other aspects of my life."

Born three decades ago in Oklahoma City, Oklahoma, Mat Hoffman began riding when he was barely old enough to walk. He joined the freestyle BMX circuit at the age of thirteen, and within two years was one of the top amateur vert riders in the world. At sixteen he turned professional.

By 1991, when he was just nineteen, Mat was the clear king of freestyle BMX. He didn't just win competitions—he redefined them. Mat routinely did tricks that no one had ever seen before.

A winner of ten world championships and two X Games gold medals, Mat continues to earn the nickname he's had for years: The Condor. In April 2001, for example, he set a world record by soaring 26.5 feet above a 24-foot vert quarterpipe. That means Mat and his bike were more than 50 feet above the ground!

DID YOU KNOW?

Mat accumulated so many absences from class while competing in BMX that he was asked to leave his high school at the age of fifteen. Years later, however, administrators at that same school invited Mat back to speak at a career day.

Mat stands at the top of an alternative sports business empire. He created the popular Bicycle Stunt Series, and is responsible for designing and manufacturing one of the most successful line of bikes in the world today. And the first video game bearing his stamp of approval was a best-seller.

No surprise, really. It seems that everything Mat touches turns to gold.

star profile

Martti KUOPPA

DATE OF BIRTH: NOVEMBER 1, 1978

"Riding for me is self-expression. I can't imagine doing anything else."

The best flatland stunt rider in the world today, Martti Kuoppa is an inventive and innovative athlete whose cool attitude masks an intense desire to succeed.

DID YOU KNOW?
In the summer of 2001, Martti rolled 100 meters no-footed on the front wheel of his bike. His accomplishment will be listed in the 2003 edition of the *Guinness Book of World Records*.

Martti began riding at the age of twelve in his hometown of Helsinki, Finland. He fell in love with the sport right away, and often practiced as much as seven hours a day. But Martti had obstacles to overcome, not the least of which was the long, harsh winter of his native land, which made riding almost impossible for half the year. He also suffered a number of painful injuries early in his career, including a broken nose and several broken teeth.

But Martti wasn't discouraged. He continued to train and invent new tricks. By 1998 he was one of the best flatland riders in freestyle BMX. He won his first X Games gold medal in that discipline in 2000, and repeated in 2001.

star profile

"Riding a bike has always been my dream. More than anything, I love to have fun, and I am always looking for opportunities to better myself and my career as a pro bike rider."

He's known as the Miracle Man, and with good reason. Dave Mirra does things on a bike no one else can do...things no one else would even try. He's been riding professionally for more than fifteen years now, and yet somehow he just keeps improving. Through all the bumps and bruises (and more serious injuries) that come with being one of the titans of extreme sports, Dave has endured and evolved. His gold medal in the vert competition at the 2001 Summer X Games in Philadelphia solidified Dave's reputation as the most decorated athlete in the history of the sport. He's now struck X Games gold ten times! And he's won thirteen medals overall.

DID YOU KNOW?
One of Dave's favorite television shows is VH1's "Behind the Music." Says Dave, "I love seeing what other people have gone through to get their success. It gives you respect for them."

One of the coolest things about Dave is that he excels at many types of freestyle riding. In an era of specialization, Dave remains committed to doing it all. He surprised a lot of people in the summer of 1996, when he won both the street and vert titles in his first X Games appearance. By 1999, however, after he'd swept both events for the fourth consecutive year, such excellence was expected of Dave. He was the undisputed king of freestyle BMX.

star profile

Stephen MURRAY

DATE OF BIRTH: JANUARY 9, 1980

Transworld BMX/Keith Mulligan

"Someday I'd like to be a team manager, so I could help people out. I'd love to treat riders how I want to be treated. I know what you need as a rider because I've been in competitions."

DID YOU KNOW?
Stephen started out as a BMX racer in England, and in fact was one of the better riders in the sport. He even finished second in his age group at the European Championships.

Talk about a comeback kid. Freestyle dirt jumper Stephen Murray will remember the year 2000 as one of the worst of his life. During a horrendous eight-month stretch, he suffered a series of injuries that should have put him out of the sport for good. Broken bones in his chest, shoulder, leg, wrist, and hand became part of his medical history. He also endured three concussions. No one in his right mind would have predicted that Stephen would do so well in his return in 2001. He became one of the top dirt jumpers in the world.

But that's exactly what happened. Stephen, a native of Great Britain who now lives in California, worked hard to get back in shape. Then, at the Summer X Games, he landed a double back flip to capture the gold medal. One month later, he completed an extreme sports double, winning the dirt jumping gold medal at the Gravity Games.

Consider Stephen's career back on the fast track.

star profile

Ryan NYQUIST

DATE OF BIRTH: MARCH 6, 1979

Short, but powerfully built (5-foot-6, 150 pounds), Ryan Nyquist is perhaps the most explosive rider in freestyle BMX. He's also one of the most versatile.

DID YOU KNOW?
Ryan is an aggressive, high-flying freestyle rider, but one of his favorite hobbies is decidedly low-key: sewing.

Although dirt jumping is his specialty, Ryan excels at park and vert riding, as well. At the 2000 X Games, for example, he was the only rider to qualify for the finals in all three freestyle disciplines. He wound up with a gold in dirt jumping and a bronze in park. In 2001 Ryan took a silver in dirt jumping at the X Games and a gold in street at the Gravity Games. He also captured the overall park title in the Bicycle Stunt Series.

"Remember to have fun, stay positive, and be strong."

(continued from page 15)

Well, it may have seemed like a crazy idea at first, but pretty soon Haro had a legion of followers. It helped that a major BMX magazine, where Haro worked as an illustrator, featured photographs of some of his tricks, along with instructional tips. Seemingly overnight, kids began flocking to skate parks on their bikes. They clogged streets and parking lots. The sport was riding in high gear!

2001 X Games
RESULTS

Bicycle Stunt Park
1. Bruce Crisman
2. Alistair Whitton
3. Jay Miron

Haro, meanwhile, proved to be not only a terrific and inventive athlete, but a smart businessman as well. In 1978, while still a teenager, he started his own company, Haro Bicycle Corporation. Although it began as a small business run out of Haro's bedroom, it quickly became one of the industry's top producers of high-end BMX and freestyle bikes. Haro himself spent equal amounts of time in the office and on the road, demonstrating the new

2001 X Games RESULTS

Bicycle Stunt Dirt

1. **Stephen Murray**
2. **Ryan Nyquist**
3. **T.J. Lavin**

tricks he had invented, on the equipment he manufactured. Injuries eventually forced Haro to retire from competition, but that didn't affect his enthusiasm for the sport he had nurtured. Instead, he recruited many of the top riders in BMX (most notably Mat Hoffman) and formed an all-star stable that made Haro a household name—presuming your household was into BMX.

The popularity of freestyle BMX faded in the late 1980s, but experienced a comeback a few years later, thanks to the efforts of several athletes who followed Haro's model. They started their own companies and promoted the sport themselves. Hoffman was again at

2001 Gravity Games RESULTS

Bike Dirt

1. **Stephen Murray**
2. **Todd Walkowiak**
3. **Chris Doyle**

Mat Hoffman

the forefront. Not only was he the most gifted rider in the sport, but, like Haro, he was a visionary. Hoffman soon realized that freestyle BMX needed more organization—specifi-

2001 X Games
RESULTS

BMX Vert
1. **Dave Mirra**
2. **Jay Miron**
3. **Mat Hoffman**

cally, it needed a series of events that would showcase the skill and creativity of its practitioners. With that in mind, Hoffman founded the Bicycle Stunt Series.

2001 Gravity Games
RESULTS

Bike Vert

1. Jamie Bestwick
2. Kevin Robinson
3. Simon Tabron

The Bicycle Stunt Series was all about the athletes. Contests were run by riders and judged by riders. The primary goal was to have fun and support the sport, and on both counts the series was a big success. ESPN approached Hoffman in the mid-1990s and offered him financial backing for the series in exchange for broadcast rights. This signaled not only the birth of big-time freestyle BMX, but the birth of the extreme sports culture as it is known today. In 1995 ESPN served up the first Extreme Games, and freestyle BMX was on the menu.

While it once took a backseat to mountain biking and traditional bicycle motocross, freestyle BMX is today one of the most popular alternative sports. It continues to grow and to become more diverse. Competition is conducted in street-style parks, on U-shaped vert ramps, and on dirt tracks. But it's not the venue that matters. In freestyle BMX, it's attitude and style that count the most.

Freestyle BMX on the Web:

www.bmxonline.com

www.bmx-style.com

www.mathoffman.com

CHAPTER 2

SPOTLIGHT Freestyle Motocross

Travis PASTRANA

DATE OF BIRTH: OCTOBER 8, 1983

DID YOU KNOW?
While most of his peers compete to the musical accompaniment of thrash or rap metal, Travis prefers old time rock 'n' roll. Jerry Lee Lewis is one of his favorites.

When was the first indication that Travis Pastrana was not quite like other kids? Maybe it was when he began driving a go-kart around his neighborhood in Annapolis, Maryland...at the age of two. Or perhaps the time, at age four, when he rode a two-wheel bicycle down a flight of stairs and into the basement of his house—without falling off! Or perhaps you have to go back even further. Maybe Travis, the biggest star in freestyle motocross, was just born to fly.

Unlike most kids, Travis grew up in a house where motorcycles were admired and respected, not feared. Robert Pastrana had been a motocross rider years earlier, and so he recognized and encouraged his son's natural ability. In fact, he bought Travis his first motorcycle, a one-speed Honda, before the boy even entered kindergarten. Travis still remembers the thrill he felt the first time he sat on that bike.

"Just to have an engine under you at an age when most kids are still on training wheels," he says. "It was unbelievable."

"Unbelievable" describes Travis's career thus far. He began entering, and winning, motocross races shortly

"Freestyle motocross is a very safe sport—99.9 percent of the time. It's just that with the heights and speeds we're reaching, when something goes wrong, you're going to get hurt."

after getting that first bike, and his first national championship came in 1992—when he was only nine years old. By the time he turned professional, Travis had accumulated four more national amateur championships.

Though he spends most of his time racing, it's freestyle motocross that has brought Travis fame and made him one of the most popular and successful athletes in extreme sports. He soars so much higher and farther than other riders, and completes so many tricks others won't even attempt, that it sometimes seems as though he's in a league of his own. Not only has Travis won three X Games gold medals, he's never lost a freestyle motocross event.

Despite having suffered some horrific injuries (he's broken more than two dozen bones), Travis still loves freestyle motocross, and has no plans to quit anytime soon.

"Motocross is so much fun," he says. "It's not something I could give up, no matter how much I get hurt."

CHAPTER 3

SKATEBOARDING

You may not realize it, but skateboarding is no cutting-edge sport. In fact, it's been around a long time.

A really long time.

Longer than some of your parents!

That's right—the granddaddy of alternative sports is more than forty years old. But don't worry. Age is largely a matter of attitude, and skateboarding is cooler than ever. Today's boards are lighter, sleeker, and offer better control than skateboarding's inventors could possibly have imag-

2001 X Games RESULTS

Vert

1. Bob Burnquist
2. Bucky Lasek
3. Tas Pappas

ined. And the six million people (in the United States alone) who own these boards are doing tricks that would make a gymnast light-headed. Skateparks have sprouted all over the country, and the top riders, free-form artists such as Tony Hawk, have an opportunity to earn as much money as professional athletes in more mainstream sports.

2001 X Games RESULTS

Vert Best Trick

1. Matt Dove
2. Tony Hawk
3. Bob Burnquist

Now, that's progress.

Along the way, skateboarding has known its share of troubles. It has risen to staggering heights of popularity, fallen into obscurity, and risen again. Several times. But where, and when, did it all begin?

That's a good question, and one that seems to have more than one good answer. The precise origin of skateboarding has long been a subject of debate. Some people claim that it was born near the beaches of southern California in the 1950s, when some creative surfers began attaching planks of wood to roller skates, so they'd have something to do when the ocean waves were too small. In truth, the roots of skateboarding can be traced much deeper into the past. Depression-era kids (in the 1930s) rode similar contraptions, and photos dating back to the turn of the century show children riding primitive scooter-like devices. They glued roller skates to two-by-fours, nailed a milk crate to the base, and attached handles to the crate for steering. Eventually, over the next few decades, the scooters were streamlined and replaced by what has come to be known as the skateboard.

There is no question that the first big skateboarding boom began in California, in the late 1950s and early 1960s. "Sidewalk surfers" would ride barefoot along beaches and through their new suburban neighborhoods on makeshift boards. The first skateboarding contest was held in 1964, in the parking lot of a junior high school in Hermosa Beach, California. More than a hundred people showed up to watch kids perform tricks that today would seem almost ridiculously easy. Still, it was a start. Pretty soon there were dozens of companies manufacturing skateboards. ABC's *Wide World of Sports* even televised the first national championships in 1965. That same year

2001 X Games
RESULTS

Vert Doubles
1. Tony Hawk & Andy MacDonald
2. Mike Crum & Chris Gentry
3. Mike Frazier & Neal Hendrix

2001 X Games
RESULTS

Park
1. Rodil de Araujo, Jr.
2. Kerry Getz
3. Caine Gayle

Street
1) Kerry Getz
2) Eric Koston
3) Chris Senn

Street Best Trick
1) Rick McCrank
2) Kerry Getz
3) Eric Koston

brought a cover story in *Life*, one of the most popular magazines in the world.

But there were problems, too. Skaters filled up sidewalks and parking lots. They tried to master more difficult tricks while using inferior equipment. A lot of them didn't wear safety gear. Some were seriously injured. Before long there was a backlash among parents, teachers, and the health community (the American Medical Association called skateboarding a "medical menace"). And skateboarding faded away.

For a while, anyway. In the early 1970s skateboarding made a comeback, thanks mainly to design improvements in the boards themselves. The modern skateboard was wider and had a slight upward curve, known as a "kicktail," at the rear, to give the rider more control. Suddenly it was possible to cut and turn quickly, just like you could on a surfboard. On the heels of this advancement came an equally

Tony Hawk

important development: the replacement of clay wheels with wheels made out of polyurethane. The new wheels were stronger, lighter, and more durable. Best of all, they provided better traction. As word of the advances spread, skateboarding roared back to life. Millions of the new boards were sold. The first skate parks appeared on the landscape. And where there weren't parks, kids made their own. Empty swimming pools, with their smooth sides and steep slopes, became a favorite destination, and gave birth to

(continued on page 50)

star profile

Bob BURNQUIST

DATE OF BIRTH: OCTOBER 10, 1976

"It's great to be a role model for kids. It's a noble job and a noble experience. But sometimes it gets pretty crazy, so I have to save some time for myself. I'm just Bob . . . a human . . . a brother in life."

One of the world's most accomplished vert skaters, Bob Burnquist is a quiet and philosophical man. He named his daughter Lotus, and once, when asked, "What's new?" by a reporter, responded in this way: "A new day, the breath I just took, and the clouds that float by."

Bob has the soul of an artist and the heart of a competitor, which makes him a particularly impressive skater. He's one of the few men in his sport who can perform almost any trick using either a regular or switch stance, a fact that has earned him the respect of his peers and the admiration of fans.

Bob was named Skater of the Year by *Thrasher* magazine in 1997, and was a gold medalist at the X Games in 2000 and 2001.

DID YOU KNOW?
Having grown up in São Paulo, Brazil, Bob's first language was Portuguese, which he still speaks fluently.

star profile

Matt DOVE

DATE OF BIRTH: FEBRUARY 23, 1973

"What I like about skateboarding is that it's really a super-creative thing. You can do whatever you want when you're on a skate-board. It's just a matter of coming up with an idea."

DID YOU KNOW?
Matt loves animals and has many pets. In fact, he used to work at the Baltimore Zoo, where he developed a love for reptiles, especially snakes and monitor lizards.

Matt Dove is usually a quiet, peaceful guy—which makes sense, considering his name, right? He's an accomplished painter and sculptor, and he avoids the spotlight whenever possible. But he also believes in standing up for himself. That's why he found himself at the center of a controversy at the 2001 X Games.

In the vert best trick competition, judges ruled that Matt landed his best move, a jaw-dropping Varial 720, after time had expired. Matt claimed otherwise, and eventually he was proved right. He was awarded the gold medal in his very first X Games event. But Matt was so upset by the experience that he vowed never to compete in the X Games again. If true, that would be a shame, since Matt is clearly one of the best vert riders in the world.

star profile

Kerry GETZ

DATE OF BIRTH: JUNE 10, 1975

"Skateboarders are like football players. We probably even take more of a beating than football players."

Now, this was appropriate.

When "true" street skateboarding made its official X Games debut in Philadelphia in the summer of 2001, one of the entrants was hometown favorite Kerry Getz. He'd grown up in Leighton, Pennsylvania, and settled down in Philadelphia, where he now owned a skateboard shop. Kerry was something of a local hero, so it was no surprise that X Games officials recruited him to help design the street course near City Hall. When it came time to put his reputation on the line, Kerry was up to the challenge, winning his first X Games gold medal.

DID YOU KNOW?
Although he's been skating for more than fifteen years, Kerry is a relative newcomer to the world of professional skateboarding. He entered his first event in 1997.

At 5-foot-10, 125 pounds, Kerry is so thin he appears almost frail. But he's actually a fearless and ferocious competitor who sets extremely high standards for himself. In fact, if he has a weakness, it's his temper. He's been known to throw his skateboard in disgust after missing a trick. But he's working on that, too.

Kerry was one of the top skaters at the 2001 X Games. In addition to his gold medal in street skateboarding, he took a silver in the best trick competition.

star profile

"I don't think about my age when I skate. I feel young."

DID YOU KNOW?
Hollywood may be Tony's next conquest. He already taught the actor Christian Slater how to skate for the 1986 film *Gleaming the Cube*, and now he has been invited to star in a movie about a fictional skateboarder.

To say that Tony Hawk is the greatest skateboarder in history isn't enough. He's a pioneer whose dynamic personality, extraordinary athletic ability, and shrewd business sense have helped bring extreme sports to a worldwide mainstream audience. It's not for nothing that he's often been called the "Michael Jordan of skateboarding."

By the time he was fourteen years old, Tony was the top-ranked skater in the world. He held that title for eleven years. Before graduating from high school he started a company that manufactured skateboarding equipment. That's been the story of Tony's life: he keeps working, growing, and evolving.

Although most of his time now is devoted to his family and various business interests (including the wildly popular PlayStation video games that bear his name), Tony remains one of the most visible men in skateboarding. He takes part in tours and exhibitions, and occasionally comes out of retirement to show the younger generation how it's done. At the 2001 X Games, for example, Tony teamed up with Andy McDonald to win a gold medal in the vert doubles competition.

So don't expect the Hawk to be grounded just yet.

star profile

Eric KOSTON

DATE OF BIRTH: APRIL 29, 1975

"I don't like restricting myself to one type of style. I would get bored with that."

In the last few years, no street skater has been more consistent than Eric Koston. The 6-foot, 160-pound Californian won gold medals at the World Championships, the Gravity Games and the X Games in 2000, a stunning hat trick that led to him being named Skateboarder of the Year.

DID YOU KNOW?

Eric looks like the coolest guy in the world when he's skating. But he's no different than anyone else when it comes to feeling the pressure of competition. In fact, Eric was so nervous before his first run at the 2001 Gravity Games that he was actually sick to his stomach. Of course, that didn't stop him from winning.

While it would have been nearly impossible for Eric to improve on that performance in 2001, he remained one of the top athletes in his sport. He repeated as Gravity Games champion, and took a pair of medals at the X Games. With a busy competitive schedule and business responsibilities that include his own clothing company, Eric doesn't have a lot of free time. An athletic, entertaining skater, he's also one of the most sought-after performers in the skateboarding video industry.

2001 Gravity Games RESULTS

Street
1. Eric Koston
2. Rick McCrank
3. Kyle Berard

(continued from page 39)

what later became the vert movement.

Insurance concerns caused the closing of many skate parks in the late 1970s, and by 1980 the sport had been driven underground—again. But there was no keeping it down. *Thrasher*, a magazine devoted to skateboarding, was born in 1981, and skateboarding again became wildly popular. The tricks became more complicated, the riders more athletic.

Today skateboarding stands at the forefront of the alternative sports movement. A mainstay of the X Games, skateboarding competitions are conducted in a variety of disciplines. The three most common are: vert, street, and downhill.

Vert skating is held on a U-shaped ramp (also known as a halfpipe) roughly 12 to 13 feet high. Skaters roll up and down the walls and launch

2001 Gravity Games RESULTS

Two-Man Downhill
1. Dane van Bommel
2. Gary Hardwick
3. Mark Golter

"A lot of people outside the skateboard world see that skateboarding is a good thing, and they want to be part of it. Now everybody wants a piece of it. Even, like, soda companies, you know?"
—Kerry Getz

themselves into the air to perform tricks that are evaluated by a panel of judges.

In street skating, the performers attempt tricks while negotiating a course that features a variety of jumps, rails, ramps, and other obstacles. In competition, street skating has traditionally been synonymous with park skating. That changed in 2001, when the X Games offered a "true" street competition to complement the park competition. For the first time ever, the natural obstacles of a city (in this case, Philadelphia) were incorporated into a street course.

2001 Gravity Games
RESULTS

Vert
1. Rune Gilfberg
2. Bucky Lasek
3. Andy MacDonald

Downhill skateboarding is the wildest and most dangerous of the three disciplines, since it involves racing downhill, in a squatting position, at speeds that can reach 60 miles per hour.

Now that's extreme!

Skateboarding on the Web:

www.skateboardermag.com

www.skateboard.com

www.unitedskate.com

CHAPTER 4

SPOTLIGHT In-Line Skating

Fabiola Da SILVA

DATE OF BIRTH: JUNE 18, 1979

The small (5-foot-2, 110 pounds) in-line skater from São Paulo, Brazil, doesn't look very intimidating. But put Fabiola Da Silva on a vert ramp, and she's a force of nature.

A multiple gold medalist at the X Games and Gravity Games, Fabiola is easily the best female in-line skater in the world. In fact, she's so good that she often competes against men. Her talent even prompted the Aggressive Skaters Association to introduce the "Fabiola Rule," which gives women the opportunity to qualify for the men's finals in ASA-sanctioned vert events. It comes as no great surprise to learn that Fabiola has taken advantage of this opportunity. In addition to winning dozens of women's championships, she's been a top-ten finisher in several men's events.

DID YOU KNOW?
When it comes to safety, Fabiola wants every advantage she can get. Her sport is risky enough as it is. So Fabiola has this bit of advice for her fans: "Wearing safety equipment is a must!"

"One day, I want to be as good as the guys," Fabiola explains. "I'm just pushing myself. Maybe other girls will see me doing it and get interested."

Girls aren't the only ones watching. This is an athlete who is so famous and admired in her native

"I hate it when guys say girls can't do things. I want to show that girls can do anything they want to do."

country that she doesn't even need a last name. As with the legendary Brazilian soccer players Pele and Ronaldo, fans and the media refer to her simply by her first name: Fabiola. Or, even more appropriately, Fabby.

As in . . . "fabulous."

How else to describe a woman who captured her first X Games gold medal in 1996, less than a year after putting on a pair of skates for the first time? Since then Fabiola has become the queen of in-line skating, winning gold medals at the X Games in 1997, 1998, 2000, and 2001.

CHAPTER 5

SNOWBOARDING

There was a time when snowboarding really was an alternative sport. Its audience was made up largely of young, hardcore kids dressed in baggy clothes more suitable for skateboarding than snowboarding. Skiers were baffled by the new sport and its followers. They were annoyed by the prospect of sharing their precious powder with a bunch of surfers who appeared to have gotten lost on their way to the beach. And they weren't alone in their contempt. In fact, it wasn't all that long ago that it was hard to find a ski resort that welcomed snow-

2001 X Games
RESULTS

Men's Snowboarder X
1. Scott Gaffney
2. Mark Schulz
3. Seth Wescott

boarders with open arms. In 1985, for example, there were more than six hundred ski areas in the United States, but only thirty-nine of them permitted the use of snowboards.

2001 X Games
RESULTS

Women's Snowboarder X
1. Line Oestveld
2. Erin Simmons
3. Amy Johnson

Why so much resistance? Fear of the unknown, perhaps. Change never comes without a fight. And, to be fair, it should be pointed out that some snowboarders in those early days went out of their way to provoke the skiing community. They rode hard and fast, and sometimes out of control. There were daily complaints about snowboarders cutting off skiers on the slopes, or jumping ahead in lift lines. For a while there, an all-out confrontation seemed unavoidable.

But that's all changed. In the year 2002 there are more than three million snowboarders in the United States alone (and many million more around the globe), and they won't have any trouble finding a place to ride this winter. All across the country, there is abundant evidence that the turf war was settled long ago. Ski resorts that once greeted boarders with

2001 X Games
RESULTS

Men's Slopestyle
1. Kevin Jones
2. Todd Richards
3. Jussi Oksanen

hostility and rejection are now rolling out the welcome mat. Gone are the days when snowboarding was practiced only by a handful of restless and sometime reckless kids. Today snowboarding is big business, its outlaw image replaced by one of fun and adventure.

The sport's biggest stars, world-class boarders like Shannon Dunn and Terje Haakonsen, get paid a lot of money—and not just when they win competitions. Like the best and most famous athletes in any sport, they have endorsement deals with equipment manufacturers and other sponsors. Some people might call that selling out, but the truth is, it's a healthy sign. Because of snowboarding's success, a generation of kids has embraced a sport that barely existed two decades ago. Many of them skip skiing and go right to boarding. And you want to know what's really cool? Their parents are asking for lessons!

So...where did this all begin? The roots of snowboarding can be traced at least as far back as the

(continued on page 70)

star profile

Tara DAKIDES

DATE OF BIRTH: AUGUST 20, 1975

"I don't like being scared...and I don't like thinking that I'm not going to do something just because I'm scared of it."

Just try to find a tougher athlete than Tara Dakides. Her long blond hair, bright eyes, and model looks tend to mask an intensity unmatched in the world of extreme sports.

DID YOU KNOW?
An avid reader and writer, Tara keeps a notebook with her whenever she travels, and often writes poems about her experiences.

No snowboarder has consistently flown higher than Tara over the past five years. She's won four X Games gold medals—two in big air and two in slopestyle. She also captured the big air world championship in 2000. But snowboarding is only one of Tara's many extreme interests. She's been skateboarding since she was a little kid, and she's surfed some of the biggest waves in the world. And, more recently, she's taken up motocross.

Shannon DUNN

DATE OF BIRTH: NOVEMBER 26, 1972

"It's amazing how snowboarding has grown. It's become a mainstream sport."

Growing up in the ski resort town of Steamboat Springs, Colorado, Shannon Dunn had easy access to some of the best trails in North America. But she was sixteen years old before she even tried snowboarding. This was 1988, the first year boarders were allowed at Steamboat. Shannon had been a promising young downhill racer with no real desire to change sports—until her brother talked her into renting a snowboard one afternoon. Shannon spent most of that day facedown in the snow.

"I went right back the next day and rented the same board again," Shannon remembers. "Then I went out and bought a board. I just loved it. I can't tell you exactly why. Maybe it was because I was burned out on skiing, and this was something new and totally different."

DID YOU KNOW?

Shannon enjoys rock climbing, swimming, tennis, mountain biking, and surfing. In fact, if she weren't a snowboarder, Shannon says she'd like to be a professional surfer.

A halfpipe gold medalist in both the X Games (1997) and Gravity Games (2000), Shannon is one of the most successful freestyle riders in the world. Although she likes to compete, Shannon tries to balance her schedule with public speaking engagements, photo shoots, and video appearances. But perhaps her favorite activity is backcountry riding, where there are no judges and no clocks—just Shannon and her snowboard, and lots of unbroken snow.

star profile

Terje HAAKONSEN

DATE OF BIRTH: OCTOBER 1, 1974

"I had much more fun playing with the board. I could do more with the terrain than I could do on skis."

Widely regarded as the greatest snowboarder in history, Terje Haakonsen has been breaking barriers and redefining his sport for more than a decade. He grew up near Oslo, Norway, and displayed exceptional athletic ability from an early age.

While soccer was his first love, skiing was a close second. But when he borrowed a neighbor's snowboard one afternoon, thirteen-year-old Terje knew he'd found his calling.

"I had much more fun playing with the board," he recalls. "I could do more with the terrain than I could do on skis."

With help from Norway's top boarder, Einar Lofthus, who took the teenager under his wing, Terje quickly ascended to the professional ranks. Combining the athleticism of a soccer player with the agility of a gymnast, Terje soon mastered some of the hardest tricks in freestyle snowboarding. And then he began creating new ones. In 1992, at the age of seventeen, all of Terje's hard work paid off. He won his first world championship in the halfpipe! Since then he's accumulated more trophies and praise than anyone in the sport, including two more world championships and five European titles.

DID YOU KNOW?

When Terje first started snowboarding, he did not have the support of his parents, who believed the sport was dangerous. So he paid for his own equipment using money he earned cutting lawns.

star profile

Shaun PALMER

DATE OF BIRTH: NOVEMBER 14, 1968

"When I want to win something, I can win it. I'm mentally stronger than any athlete out there in any sport I do."

A self-described "speed freak," Shaun Palmer likes to live on the edge. This is a man who has tried just about every extreme sport there is, and has excelled at most of them. Downhill mountain biking, skiing, snowmobile racing, motocross, even auto racing—Shaun has won major events in each of these activities. Maybe that's why he's considered the Iron Man of alternative sports.

DID YOU KNOW?
Shaun's other passion in life is music. In fact, he sings and plays guitar for a punk-metal band called the Elkos.

But if there is one sport for which Shaun is most well known, it's snowboarding. The 5-foot-9, 170-pound Californian won his first world championship when he was only sixteen years old. That was half a lifetime ago, but Shaun has shown no hint of slowing down. At thirty-three, he has three X Games gold medals in boardercross under his belt, and remains one of the best riders in the world.

star profile

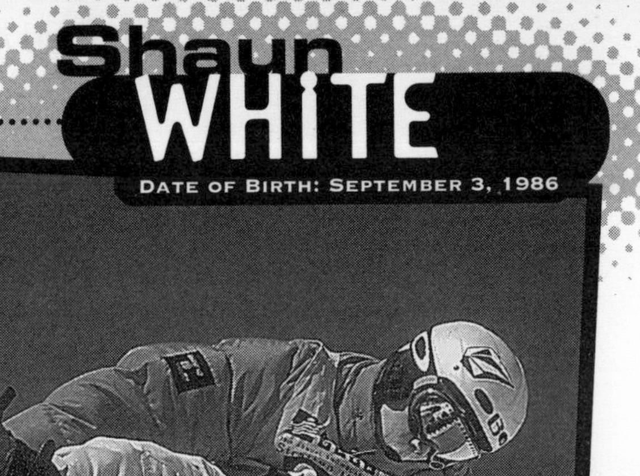

"Sometimes I get a little nervous, especially in big competitions. But I just try to have fun and do the best I can."

Not since the early days of Terje Haakonsen's career has any snowboarder received the kind of praise that's been showered on Shaun White. The fifteen-year-old kid with flaming red hair and acrobatic moves has taken the snowboarding world by storm. And deservedly so. This, after all, is a true child star. Want proof? Well, consider that Shaun won his first overall amateur title when he was just eight years old. After defending that crown four more times, he turned professional in 1998—at the age of twelve! Since then his tiny, twisting form has become a familiar sight to snowboarding fans all over the globe.

DID YOU KNOW?
Shaun is also a gifted skateboarder. In fact, he skates as much as three hours a day, and says that he might one day give pro skating a shot.

It's kind of funny—they call Shaun "Future Boy" on the pro snowboarding tour, because he has limitless potential. But if you watch him soar out of a halfpipe and land a McTwist, you'll know the truth: for Shaun White, the future is now.

(continued from page 59)

Terje Haakonsen

early 1920s, when children in snow-covered New England created something that looked like snowboards out of barrel staves. And there have been tales of soldiers in Europe during World War I (1914 to 1918) passing the time by sliding down icy hillsides on makeshift snowboards. But if credit is to be given to one man for creating the modern snow-board, then that man is Sherman Poppen.

Poppen was an inventor by trade, so he was inclined to look at things differently than most people. On Christmas morning in 1965 Poppen walked out

"In most sports, it's all about the competition, but there's a different approach in snowboarding. I like contests— it's a way to push your mental and physical limits. But I don't like to do only contests, because it limits your riding and your ability to have fun with the sport."
—Shannon Dunn

2001 X Games
RESULTS

Women's Slopestyle
1. Jamie MacLeod
2. Shannon Dunn
3. Marni Yamada

of his Michigan home and stared at a hillside blanketed with snow. For some reason, Poppen thought the hill resembled a wave, and he began to imagine what it might be like to ride that wave on a surfboard. Of course, that wasn't possible. But maybe, Poppen thought, there was a way to modify a surfboard in such a way that it could be used on snow.

Within a few hours he was standing at the top of that hill, the world's first snowboard beneath his feet. It was crude and unattractive, made out of two skis nailed together. But it worked! And that's all that really mattered. Poppen's young daughters loved the new toy. So did other kids in their neighborhood. Poppen tinkered with his board. He made it faster, lighter. A rope was added to the tip for balance and maneuverability. Pretty soon

2001 X Games
RESULTS

Men's Superpipe
1. Dan Kass
2. Tommy Czeschin
3. Ross Powers

2001 X Games
RESULTS

Women's Superpipe
1. **Shannon Dunn**
2. **Natasza Zurek**
3. **Fabienne Reuteler**

word of Poppen's invention spread. Of course, it didn't have a name yet, so no one knew what to call it. Poppen took care of that problem by combining the words "snow" and "surfer," and before long the "Snurfer" was flying out of stores all over the country (more than a million of the boards were sold).

Poppen's work had a big influence on the winter sports industry. Others followed in his footsteps (or tracks, as the case may be), and over time the snowboard evolved into what it is today: a sleek, aerodynamic board that can be ridden safely by almost anyone—from pre-schoolers to senior citizens.

Of course, for the truly adventurous, it's also a vehicle that can be used to defy gravity. Whether racing down the side of a mountain (in events such as boarder-

2001 X Games
RESULTS

Ultracross
1. **Shaun Palmer & Hiroomi Takizawa**
2. **Jason Evans & Isidor Gruener**
3. **Pontus Staahlkloo & Matt Murphy**

cross—also known as snowboarder X), creating new moves in freestyle contests (halfpipe and superpipe), or merely catching big air, world-class snowboarders are known for their courage and skill. Watching a halfpipe competition at the X Games or the Gravity Games, you can't help but be awestruck by the skills on display.

Why, it's enough to make you want to trade in your skis.

Snowboarding on the Web:

www.snowboarding.com

www.snowboardermag.com

www.kidznsnow.com

CHAPTER 6

SPOTLIGHT

Surfing

Kelly SLATER

DATE OF BIRTH: FEBRUARY 11, 1972

DID YOU KNOW?
One of Kelly's favorite sports is golf. He didn't start playing until the late 1990s, but already has a single-digit handicap.

The poster boy of modern surfing, Kelly Slater grew up in Cocoa Beach, Florida, an area not typically associated with big waves. Great surfers come from California and Hawaii, he was told. But he didn't listen. Instead, Kelly spent countless hours in the water, practicing until his skin turned to leather and his arms and legs ached. He was a student of surfing, more serious than his West Coast rivals, and eventually his hard work paid off.

Kelly was fiercely competitive, even in grade school. He hated to lose—at anything—and that desire to succeed helped make him one of the greatest surfers in history.

"I used to win on anger," Kelly once told *Outside* magazine. "I'd get fired up for anyone who had beaten me in a heat, anyone who said anything negative in a magazine. I tried not just to win heats, but to dominate them. I wanted to smother the other guys."

Kelly even kept a log of his competitions, in which he'd write descriptions of each heat. Sometimes he'd write "too impatient," or "catching too

"The overall level of surfing should be twenty percent higher. People should focus more on basic form, the shoulder line and balance, which no one talks about. "

many waves." While other surfers rolled through events blindly, Kelly was determined to analyze his performances. In that way he'd be less likely to repeat his mistakes.

Obviously, it worked, for Kelly won six world titles in the 1990s. With movie-star looks, he became more popular than the sport itself. He sold millions of posters and video games, modeled for top designers, and landed huge advertising deals. He even had a recurring role on the television series *Baywatch*.

More recently Kelly found a new challenge: surfing big waves on customized surfboards with footstraps. Imagine snowboarding on water and you get the idea.

"You can do floaters on 10-foot waves," Kelly says enthusiastically of the new equipment. "You have so much more control of the board."

With Kelly giving his stamp of approval, don't be surprised if it catches on.

CHAPTER 7

WAKEBOARDING

Just think about the inspiration behind wakeboarding, the combination of factors that helped make it what it is today: one of the fastest growing alternative sports. There are more than four million wakeboard enthusiasts around the world, an incredible number considering the sport is really still in its infancy. So you have to wonder: Is this what Tony Finn envisioned?

Finn was a surfer from San Diego, California, in the 1980s whose hunger for new challenges extended beyond the usual quest for the perfect wave. It wasn't unusual then to see the occasional surfer being towed behind a boat, or dragged through the water while holding a long rope attached to a truck on shore. But those were purely diversions for the athletes involved. It was Finn who came up with the idea of creating a board specifically designed for a new sport—a combination of water skiing and surfing.

His hybrid creation, the Skurfer, looked like a little surfboard, and was meant to be pulled behind a power boat. The rider would perform surf-like tricks along the wake of the boat. Finn's invention didn't catch on right away. Critics felt the sport lacked the speed and excitement of surfing, and the control of water skiing. It borrowed heavily from those sports, but was inferior to both—until the summer of 1985.

2001 X Games
RESULTS

Men's

1. Danny Harf
2. Darin Shapiro
3. Erik Ruck

It was then that Finn added foot straps to the Skurfer. The effect was dramatic. Suddenly "skiboarding," as it was called, was a sport that made sense. As with bindings on snowboards, the foot straps gave riders more control over their equipment. Instead of slipping and sliding on the water, they could now do a variety of new tricks. What had been an interesting but awkward activity now became the coolest of water sports. It was easy to learn—easier even than water skiing. And for those who craved speed and height, it was ideal. Roaring behind a power boat, with his feet locked into place, an aggressive, acrobatic rider could launch himself off the wake and catch reasonably big air, just as if he were snowboarding.

2001 X Games
RESULTS

Women's
1. Dallas Friday
2. Emily Copeland
3. Tara Hamilton

The Skurfer (and various copycat models), however, still couldn't bring skiboarding to a mainstream audience. The early models were narrow and overly buoyant; they also lacked durability. But that all changed in 1990, with the introduction of the first Hyperlite boards, designed and marketed by a businessman named Herb O'Brien, the owner of H.O. Sports, a leading water ski manufacturer. The Hyperlite boards were strong yet light, and not so buoyant that a rider couldn't submerge it and start in deep water. This made the sport much more

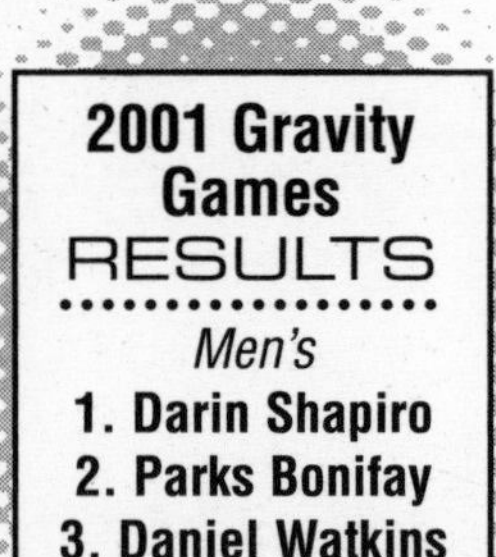

accessible, and before long the wakeboarding movement took flight. Its popularity soared, and so did the more accomplished practitioners of the sport. They cut effortlessly through the water, completed breathtaking somersaults, and used jumps and ramps to catch air.

Wakeboarding (as it became known in the early 1990s) was a fun sport to watch and an easy sport to learn. Advances in technology made it even better. The narrow, surfboard-like design of early boards was replaced in 1993, when a fatter, twin-tipped model was introduced. That design is more balanced, with a fin at each end of the board, and remains the standard today.

Of course, every new sport needs an organizing body and a professional tour before it can claim legitimacy, and wakeboarding now has both. The World Wakeboard Association, founded by Redmon in 1989, oversees all rules and competitions, including the Pro Wakeboard Tour.

(continued on page 94)

Tara Hamilton

star profile

Parks BONIFAY

DATE OF BIRTH: SEPTEMBER 30, 1981

"The most important thing I've learned about competing is to have fun."

With the nickname "Wonder Boy," Parks Bonifay has a lot to live up to. So far, he's met the challenge.

Parks is in the *Guinness Book of World Records* as the youngest water skier ever (six months, twenty-nine days). He was just twelve years old when he started wakeboarding, and only fourteen when he won his first X Games gold medal in 1996. He struck gold again in 1999. He finished that year as the top-ranked freestyle rider on the pro wakeboarding tour. Parks was also ranked number one in freeride in 1998 and 2001.

DID YOU KNOW?
Athleticism runs in the Bonifay family. Parks's brother, Shane, is also a world-class wakeboarder.

DATE OF BIRTH: SEPTEMBER 6, 1986

"Wakeboarding is so much fun. I get to travel and hang out with my friends. I love it!"

The word "prodigy" gets tossed around a bit too easily sometimes, but it certainly fits 5-foot, 100-pound Dallas Friday. The teen sensation with one of the coolest names in alternative sports has been wakeboarding less than three years, but already she's making waves. She made her X Games debut in 2000, taking a silver medal in freeride. The following year, at the age of fourteen, she swept gold at the X Games and Gravity Games.

Not bad for someone who didn't set foot on a wakeboard until June of 1999. Dallas had been a serious gymnast up to that point, winning regional and state championships in Florida. But the long hours of training took their toll, and by the time she was introduced to wakeboarding by her older brother, Dallas was ready for a change. She embraced the new sport with the same energy and dedication she had displayed as a gymnast, and before long she was successfully competing against the top pros in the world.

DID YOU KNOW?

Dallas has two nicknames. The first is "Little D," because she reminds people of Darin Shapiro, one of the top riders on the men's tour. The other, she jokes, is "Houston Thursday."

Today Dallas remains the youngest competitor on the pro tour, but no one treats her like a little girl. In fact, when medals are handed out, she often stands tallest.

star profile

DATE OF BIRTH: JANUARY 16, 1982

"This is the only sport I've ever really stuck with. I think my parents are happy I've found something that I like a lot."

DID YOU KNOW?
Home schooled as a teen, Tara is now working toward a business degree in college.

Wakeboarding's first female superstar, Tara Hamilton came to the sport in 1996, at the age of fourteen. She was an athletic girl who had tried a lot of other sports—soccer, tennis, diving, gymnastics—but nothing had really captured her interest. Wakeboarding did. Tara entered her first professional event in 1997 and surprised herself by reaching the finals. That same year she won a gold medal at the X Games.

Tara was easily at the top of women's wakeboarding for the next three years. In 2000 she won another X Games gold medal and was ranked number one on the pro tour. A fractured bone in her foot slowed Tara at the start of 2001, but she still managed to win a silver medal at the Gravity Games and a bronze at the X Games.

star profile

Danny HARF

Date of Birth: October 15, 1984

"Don't get upset when you're trying to learn new tricks. Just have fun."

A lot was expected of junior world champion Danny Harf when he jumped to the professional ranks in 2000. And he didn't disappoint. With confidence and poise usually seen only in more mature athletes, Danny cracked the pro tour's top ten and was named Rookie of the Year. But that was merely a glimpse of things to come.

DID YOU KNOW?
Danny's sister, Lauren, is also a wakeboarder. She was a top-ten finisher at both the X Games and Gravity Games in 2001.

At the 2001 Summer X Games in Philadelphia, Danny turned in a stunning performance to upset Darin Shapiro. The defending X Games champ had executed a 900 (two-and-a-half full spins) to take the lead just minutes earlier, so Danny had to be nearly flawless on his final run in order to have any chance of winning. Rather than giving up, Danny treated the crowd of 7,000 lining the Schuylkill River to "the best run of my life."

Rest assured, though—there will be many more like it. Danny's just getting started.

Darin SHAPIRO

DATE OF BIRTH: OCTOBER 25, 1973

"I always try to do the best that I can, and sometimes that focus may appear as being too serious. But that doesn't mean I don't enjoy what I'm doing."

The most successful rider in the history of wakeboarding, Darin Shapiro was born in Fort Lauderdale, Florida. He played a lot of sports as a kid, most notably BMX and surfing. It wasn't until his senior year in high school, when he was seventeen years old, that he tried wakeboarding. Of course, that was 1991, roughly the same time that the sport's popularity began to blossom. And Darin quickly became it's most skilled practitioner.

An aggressive, creative rider, Darin won his first World Wakeboard Association pro tour championship in 1992. Since then he's been the tour's top-ranked, year-end rider on five occasions. Darin has also been a fixture at the X Games, winning five medals, including golds in 1997 and 2000. He was also Gravity Games champion in 2000 and 2001.

DID YOU KNOW?
Darin is a big fan of music. He even has a recording studio in his home in Orlando, Florida.

(continued from page 82)

"I like being part of a sport that's really progressing. There are so many opportunities to be innovative, and to push the standards of wakeboarding." —Danny Harf

Wakeboarding has been a part of the world's biggest alternative sports festival, the X Games, since 1996, but its popularity has mushroomed in recent years. Little more than a curiosity in those early days, wakeboarding in 2001 drew some of the biggest X Games crowds. And why not? Fans lining the Schuylkill River were treated to a new and improved version of the sport, this one blending not only surfing and water skiing, but also skateboarding. That's right . . . skateboarding. Wakeboarding's new look featured a course that was designed to copy images of

2001 Gravity Games RESULTS

Women's
1. Dallas Friday
2. Tara Hamilton
3. Christy Smith

a street skating park, complete with ramp sliders and horizontal siderails. The fans ate it up, cheering wildly at the tricks of such young stars as Dallas Friday and Danny Harf. If their championship performances were any indication, the future of wakeboarding is bright indeed!

Wakeboarding on the Web:

www.wwa.com
(World Wakeboard Association)

www.prowakeboardtour.com

www.wakeboardingmag.com